This is a work of non-fiction. I have tried to recreate events, locales and conversations from Yuna's memoirs. In order to maintain their anonymity in some instances I have changed the names of individuals and places, I may have changed some identifying characteristics and details such as physical properties, occupations and places of residence.

DADDY'S CURSE: A HARROWING TRUE STORY OF AN EIGHT-YEAR-OLD GIRL HUMAN SEX TRAFFICKING AND ORGANIZED CRIME SURVIVOR

This book contains strong language, explicit violence and scenes of a sexual nature

Editing by Stephanie Hoogstad

Narrated by Nunt. R

Designed by Rebecacovers

Beautiful minds inspire others

Written by Luke. G. Dahl.

First edition. December 12, 2017.

DADDY'S CURSE

A Harrowing True Story of an Eight-Year-Old Girl Human Trafficking and Organized Crime Survivor

Luke. G. Dahl

Luke. G. Dahl

Contents

CHAPTER ONE

Taken

I was born in Mongolia, a landlocked country in East Asia.

When they came for me – my kidnappers – I was eight years old. It was supposed to be a quiet day as usual with the clear blue sky beaming with brightness while my family and I rested within the thin walls of our small country home on the steeps.

I could remember Father then. His name was Yeke. I felt he was the tallest man there was in the entire world. He had eyes with unmistakable glints of both sadness and hope and didn't speak much. Despite his constant silence, it was obvious how often he was unsatisfied with the situation at home. With the little that he earned, he had to cater for me, my mother and my little sister, Saran. It seemed like much to do for

4

him and he was too emotional to hide this from everyone. His constant sighs and loose shoulders every evening was enough to give him out.

That afternoon, Father and I had taken a walk as we seldom did and returned home, a bit exhausted. Saran should be four at the time and being the youngest, she got most of Mother's attention. Mother sat on a wooden chair in the sitting room, a smiling Saran on her thigh, and only acknowledged our presence with a brief smile. She nodded slowly as Father poured himself a cup of water, gulped down half of it and gave the rest to me. I thought she was going to call for me, but her gaze dropped to Saran once more, giving her all the attention.

Like the most first child, I didn't like that Mother always wanted to please Saran. Father had fallen into one of the chairs and had closed his eyes, dozing off immediately. Seeing that I wasn't getting the least attention from either of them, I finished my water and slipped out of the house, preferring the vast view of the grassland outside to the brooding silence inside.

I was a quiet child then too, just like Father, but this was because I always thought I could keep to myself and make myself happy by playing with the grasses or butterflies during the summer.

Keeping to myself was why my kidnappers successfully separated me from my family and country home for more than twelve years now.

Enjoying the view a few feet from our home, at first, I heard the twigs of sticks, the rustling of leaves and then steady footsteps, but I was too young to sense danger – as imminent as it was. Even when two men suddenly grabbed me by both arms and placed a palm over my lips, I couldn't struggle much. I was only baffled, and a bit shook with the revelation that I was being dragged further and further away from what I knew to be home.

Both men were too careful to let go of me. They held on strongly to my arms and feet, their fingers digging deep and already causing bruises to my skin.

"Father!" I was able to mutter eventually, my shaking voice doing no justice to the cry for help that I wanted.

There weren't just two men anymore. There was a third on a horseback a mile away from home, waiting for them with two other horses. The two men pushed me atop one of the horses immediately, one of them climbing behind me and holding me strongly in place. He smelled of urine and alcohol. I watched, disoriented, as the second man hopped on his horse too and strongly rode ahead, urging the rest to do the same.

They rode north, farther away from home and leaving only dust behind.

"Ride faster." I heard the man in the front yell. "Her family could notice her gone anytime!"

I wanted to glance back at the family I knew but a strong arm still held me in place. I could imagine now, my parents heading out of the house, terrified and troubled by my absence. Mother would probably wail my name, searching everywhere while father tried to calm her down. Eventually, staring north into the distant horizon, they would notice the specks of dust from the hooves of horses – the only proof that I was once a little girl that lived in their home.

To me, the dust felt like a thick wall between that which I knew and the destiny that waited for me after my kidnap.

If only I was old enough to know I would never be happy again.

Mongolia, as I knew it then, was located between Russia to the North and China to the south. It had vast grassland steeps, forested areas, very little arable lands, harsh regional climate and over two million, five hundred people, amongst which majority were Buddhists.

As hours passed by and as the men on horsebacks rode on, I was leaving all those behind. Tears dripped down my cheeks, but my captors were least concerned about it. We had ridden six hours farther from my home, the sky totally dark except for the glinting dots of stars, when we were joined by trains of riders with guns strapped to their thighs and boots. There were more men on horses and additional wagons fastened to a few horses. The wagons had cages with iron bars and some children, probably the same age that I was or a few years older, were locked in them.

During the rest of the journey, I learned that the children immediately thrown into the wagons were obviously the children that gave the men tough times.

Most of us were females, so we were easily subdued but some wanted to go back home and sometimes took a run for it. They were easily caught, beaten and thrown into the cages without food for days.

When we met the new riders and their train, it became obvious that the men that took me were part of a vicious kidnapping group. They took us from our parents and neither of us knew what was in store for us. They said nothing to me or to the rest of the children. As we rode the first day, they offered nothing except water and sordid scorns. I was later put into the wagon cages with the rest of the children and silently did everyone rides on, the tears in our eyes being the only connection I felt with everyone else.

There are vast desert lands in Mongolia and our captors seemed to know which route exactly to take to avoid encountering people or arousing suspicion to the kind of train they led. I didn't know what town we turned to or the borders that were crossed as we rode for two days. Our captors kept moving fast. They only stopped twice a day to do a head count of everyone as well as to feed us with as little as possible. I could remember that at some point, I guessed that they only fed us that little to make us too weak to escape or fight them – as if we could.

The second day, while we stopped over during midday in the middle of a desert, one of us spoke to the rest for the first time. I never knew his real name, but I knew he had curly black hair and a pointy nose like Italians in soap operas. He looked older than the rest of us too – probably eleven or twelve. I had noticed him earlier in the cage, always having his eyes focused on the route that the horses took; the other wagons with cages and on the men as they changed direction and took turns to feed us.

"Hey." He called out softly to the rest of us in the cage. Apart from him and I, there was six other girls and a boy.

None of us gave him our attention at first but he whispered again and got half of our attention.

"I think we can make a run for it again." He whispered, his eyes glaring into each of our eyes.

He had all our attention now. Some of the girls shook their heads in fright while the other boy looked on indifferently. For me, I wondered briefly what he meant by *make a run for it, again.* Had they done it before? Was that why they were fed far lesser than I was fed and had been in the cage longer than I have?

"I didn't take note of what they did before. We just ran as soon as we saw the chance. It was why we were caught. I am smarter now. We are."

The boy was still speaking and although the rest said nothing, it was obvious they were listening to him and either agreeing or disagreeing with him with their silence.

"What do you think, Newcomer? You think we should escape if I have got a new plan?"

It took a while before I realized the attention in the cage had shifted to me. At that moment, I also realized that it seemed that the rest of the children were already familiar with each other. The older one obviously led their small group since their kidnap and I was the last entry – the last to join the train of captives. He was also asking me a question that I had no reasonable response to. It had been two days and I was still shaken that we went farther and farther from my home.

"I...I...I don't know." I finally responded when no one would do anything but stare at me. "Have you done this before...I mean, escape?" I also asked.

I felt as if I asked him a stupid question, despite how obvious the answer was. He didn't mind though. His eyes scanned our surrounding again to be sure no one was listening to us before he edged closer and offered his hand for a handshake.

"We have had a few tough days." I heard him whisper as I slowly shook his hand. "We all haven't had time to get to know each other. Besides you are Altantsetseg,

Chinua, Erhi, and Khulan. That is Jullian, the only boy apart from me."

I let my eyes trail his eyes to the faces of everyone he introduced. I nodded to each person too, having no idea if I was to say anything to them. When he was through, he pointed to his own chest and said, "You can just call me Od. What's your name?"

"Yuna," I replied, already gaining a little composure.

"Okay, Yuna. To answer your previous question, we tried to escape once...."

"But we were caught." Altantsetseg, one of the girls interrupted suddenly. "We should stay where we are."

Altantsetseg had a tiny voice. She had her face to the floor as she spoke, thereby having her wavy black hair cover most of her face. I noticed for the first time that her fingers clutched the fingers of another girl – the one Od had introduced as Chinua. They both had wavy black hair and looked alike, although Chinua's hair was a bit shorter than Altantsetseg's.

"If we stay right here, we would be sold like slaves or worse maimed while our parts are sold."

Od dropped the probability of our fates unexpectedly that we all gasped at the same time. I hadn't thought of that the entire time. The others probably had...or not. How come Od was the one with all the ideas?

"How do you know they will do that to us?"

Jullian had read my mind. He hadn't said a word since Od began the conversation about our escape, but he was staring at Od with fright now.

"I heard one of the men talk about the prices for selling us according to our age," Od explained with a grimace. "They talk loudly mostly during the night after a few drinks. The other idea of selling our parts came from a movie I once saw on television."

"What movie?" Jullian asked.

"Does it matter?" Od groaned. His eyes had flown to the terrain outside the cage again and he seemed to be worried suddenly. "Tonight is when we escape." He whispered. "One of the men said we might be crossing over to a nearby town by sundown. The town is where we run to. I am running, with or without you guys."

I was about to ask how he planned to get all seven of us to escape for example, without getting caught almost immediately but footsteps suddenly resounded around us. We heard the neighing of horses too, signaling that we were about to move again.

Once again, they were taking each one of us towards a totally unknown destination and farther away from our families.

The entire afternoon, none of us said anything in our cages. I sometimes stared through the iron bars at the other wagons, wondering if the children in the cages were also as anxious as we were in ours.

There weren't any firm decisions yet, but it was obvious that some of us were really considering running as soon as there was an opportunity at sundown. Sundown was when our captors would stop to feed us. The cage would be opened to allow us to step down and sit around at a spot to eat our dinner. We were always watched, and I was still confounded how any sane person would want to use the hour to escape. The men had guns. They could fire at us if we were too much of a trouble or worse if we were to get away and tell anyone about their vicious business.

"Are you thinking about it?"

Julian's whisper was faint, but I caught on that he was talking to me when I noticed the sad smile on his face as he stared at me.

"Thinking about what?" I whispered back.

"Tonight." He simply whispered.

"Yes." There was no point lying about it. "Are you?" I asked.

"Yes." He whispered too.

That was all. Neither of us said anything else. We, like the rest, were lost in various thoughts about the possibility of freeing ourselves and what could happen next.

I spent the next hour thinking about my mother and my sister, Saran, to distract myself. I could remember how fond of my mother Saran was. Mother loved her too. She loved me too. She held each of our hands whenever she went to the grocery store and would have us hold on to each other's hands like a lovely family. Father played with us sometimes too. He would come home with fruits sometimes and share them equally.

I missed all that since I had been taken. I missed even having to hate Saran for having all of Mother's attention. Imagining Mother's, Father's and Saran's smiling faces in my head; I rested my head on one of the cage's iron, closed my eyes and slept.

I dreamt briefly of the day I was kidnapped. This time around, I could hear Mother's wailings in the distance. Father was yelling my name while Saran cried in fear. Everything was happening too fast; I was being taken away and I couldn't tell what was going to happen to me. Eventually, feeling helpless as if I was falling into a deep dark hole, I let a loud yell fill my throat.

I woke up then, feeling sweat dripping from my entire body. My head wasn't resting on the iron of the cage anymore. I cuddled on the floor, noticing at first how I had managed to squeeze myself in between everyone. By the looks of the cloud above me, I had been asleep for more than an hour. The clouds were dark with rays of the descending sun giving its edges a glint of orange.

When I stared around me, I noticed that Altantsetseg and Chinua were also asleep, with their fingers clutched as usual. The rest had their backs to the cage irons, lost in thought. Across where I laid, Od was staring down at me, frowning.

"You had a bad dream." He didn't ask. He simply muttered quietly as if he had been in my head the entire time, seeing the pain I could imagine my family was going through.

I didn't mutter any words back. I only nodded and raised myself to a sitting position.

"Good," Od whispered nonetheless, his eyes scanning the descending darkness around us. "Then you shouldn't see what is about to happen as anything worse."

About to happen? I realized at that moment that the wagon had stopped right before I woke up. Was it time for our dinner? Was it time for our escape? What was the plan? Why was the atmosphere suddenly tenser in the cage?

"Hey! Step away from the cage!"

Two men stepped in front of our wagon suddenly. The taller one pointed a finger at me as he spoke while the other withdrew a bunch of keys from his belt. I did as I was told. I edged further into the cage, squeezing myself with the rest who wouldn't stop shivering or groaning. The man with the bunch of keys climbed the wagon a second later and unlocked the cage. He opened the door and stepped aside, expecting us to head out to eat as we have for the past few days.

"Come on now. Chop chop! We haven't got all day." His partner on the ground urged us out.

Od and I were the first to step out and down the wagon. We silently followed the other man as he led us a few feet away from the wagon towards a small fire that had been made in the middle of an open ground.

We were close to the fire when I felt a soft tap on my palm. Od was beside me and was muttering words so quietly and fast I almost didn't catch on any phrase.

"Yuna. Listen, I will be fast with this – I already told the rest while you were asleep. The two men that would be watching us drink a lot." I heard him say. "They also get distracted since they like to talk a lot while we eat.

That's when we run. Run towards where the sun sets; that's where the nearby town is supposed to be."

I couldn't mutter a reply. I wasn't even sure I caught on each word accurately. Both men had rounded us all around the fire and had begun to serve us food in a small bowl. Whatever dinner was, I had not eaten it before. It tasted like sour soup mixed with corn. We all ate it hungrily though since we haven't been fed anything the entire day.

"You can get your own water from the jug over there. One at a time." The shorter of the two men instructed after we had all been given food.

True to Od's observation, both men slowly began to move away from us. They stayed a few feet from the fire with their back to us and began to share liquid from a pocket bottle. Their laughter also rented the air, showing how engrossed they were with their conversation.

I kept my eyes on Od. He was busy scanning everywhere with his eyes and eating at the same time.

Behind him, another fire glowed in the distance, the silhouettes of another group of children visible around it. There were three fires made in total, each group of children being watched by selected men. Years later, I assumed that the strategy by our captors at the time was to divide us in small numbers and have us watched strictly. Also, if the train was to be chased or attacked, each group could escape through various routes and confuse whosoever sought to catch them.

Eventually, Od dropped his bowl and slowly stood, watching to see if his movement would arouse any suspicion. He waited a second or two to watch again. When nothing happened, he slowly took steps towards the jug of water, also in a bid to see if he would be reprimanded. It was a smart move. As soon as he got near to the jug, one of the men glanced behind his shoulder at us and then back to his friend when he noticed that Od was only getting himself water to drink.

Staring around and confirming that we were no longer being watched, Od stared at us briefly, giving the sign that it was high time we moved.

At first, nobody moved. I froze with my bowl in my hand, wondering if it was the right thing to do. Then, the faces of Father, Mother, and Saran flashed in my head and I found myself slowly dropping the bowl to the floor and rising to my feet.

Altantsetseg, Chinua and Khulan did the same too. I didn't have the time to check if Jullian would be going through with it before heading after Od who was already running as fast and as silently as he could towards where it was apparent the sun had set.

So far, I could see Altantsetseg and Chinua behind me. Both sisters reflected the same anxiety and fear that I felt. They kept glancing behind their shoulders and despite how dark it was becoming, I could see their eyes dance nervously in their sockets.

"Run, Yuna. Run."

Od was urging me on as much as he could. He was a few feet ahead of me and seemed to disappear into the darkness with each step. We were on a desert land in the middle of nowhere. I could only make out the rays of orange color in the sky, boulders with numerous sizes around us that we had to avoid and how suddenly cold and fierce the wind had become.

The burning fire we left behind was gradually becoming a dot in the distance and I thought we could make it very far before our absence was noticed. That didn't happen. Suddenly, we heard loud groans in the distance as well as Julian's wail. It was as if he was being beaten or tortured. He should have run too, I thought, feeling sad for him. The men were probably questioning him about the direction we were running towards.

"Just keep running. We would be there faster if we never stop."

Od was doing his best to encourage us but I couldn't sense through his shaking voice that he was afraid too.

Apart from fear, there was something else. Uncertainty! Yes! He wasn't even sure where we are headed or if a nearby town existed in the first place. We could be heading deep into the desert without any possibility of ever finding our way out.

"I see them! I see them! There they are! You stop this instant!"

Voices echoed behind us. The men had seen us, despite how dark it was, and they were hot on the pursuit. If we were lucky, they would be too worried about our escape, they wouldn't think to go back and hop on a horse to get to us faster. Glancing back and seeing that they had only picked up a wood with fire, I realized we were indeed lucky.

There was already a mile distance between us and we didn't seem like we would stop any time soon. Ahead of me, Od climbed a heap of sand and I did the same, panting hard. It was getting more and more difficult to run but I told myself I wouldn't stop, not even to catch a breath. Altantsetseg and Chinua were slowing down behind me, each sister still holding on to each other's hand.

"Go! Go! Go!"

At the top of the heap, Od had waited for us. He slapped his wrist against my back, urging me down the heap, and immediately I joined him there. I kept running downwards, seeing nothing, breathing hard. Behind me, I heard Od yelling at the sisters to run faster and head down as well. A hard breeze hit me hard across my face, but I wouldn't stop heading down...I couldn't. I could finally go back home. I could see Mother and Father again.

"Stop! Stop right there or we will shoot...."

The men were nearer now. They were older and faster. Not feeding us well was a good strategy after all. We couldn't even run a few miles without them catching on fast.

I wasn't discouraged though. I noticed the downward slope that I ran wasn't ending soon but it was the least of my problem. I couldn't even make out if Od, Altantsetseg or Chinua were still running behind me. I just didn't want to go back to that cage. *You don't, Yuna. You don't.*

Suddenly, when I thought the only sound that could eventually put a string in my step was the loud beating of my heart, I heard a louder one echo around me. It sounded like...like a gunshot!

I paused for a second then, drops of sweat already rolling down my entire skin. I stared around me, shivering, lost, afraid and totally unsure of what to do. *Just keep running, Yuna,* I told myself; and I did. I could hear Od's advice echo in my ears too. I would get to the town faster if I don't stop running. It was what I was going to do – keep running.

I had taken more steps away from down the endless heap of sands when I heard another gunshot. This time around, I wasn't affected by its deafening sound. It only got me to race down faster, without a care in the world for anything except getting to the bottom of the heap and to my freedom.

Eventually, feeling my feet hitting solid rock bottom, I grinned happily and glanced behind my shoulders one last time. It felt like a wall that reached the sky now, the heap of sand. It cast around like an enemy shadow and I knew right on top of it, were the monsters that wanted me right back in the cage I had escaped from.

Preparing myself, I heaved a long sigh, turned and kept running. The last thing I heard was the echo of another gunshot before my legs gave way underneath me. I felt my body tumbling down another heap of sand. It was like the dream I had earlier. I was falling.... deep into a darkness I couldn't understand.

My head hit a rock once. I felt sand slithering into my clothing and tearing into my skin. I tasted the dust in my nostrils and in my throat. Eventually, as my body slowly began to glide down the slope, the weight of sand almost pressing my body deep into the earth, I felt darkness take over my senses as my head hit another stone.

Three gunshots, I thought before I went unconscious. Perhaps, one had luckily hit me and ended my life.

It was a fate far better than being sold off.

CHAPTER TWO

Found

I was still breathing.

I felt the dryness of my throat first before I realized that I couldn't move a muscle. My body felt as if a story building had crashed on it. My shoulders hurt. I felt piercing pain all over my neck while my backbone felt as if I had been to the coal mine. It felt difficult to flutter my eyelids open too, and after catching a few breaths first, I was finally able to do that.

My vision was blurry at first, but I was able to make out a clear morning sky above me. I could also faintly hear the chirping of forest birds. When my sight finally cleared, I noticed the soft animal skin blankets that had been spread over the area that I slept on. Short wooden walls surrounded me too, like the wagons of my captors. Frightened, I totally forgot about the piercing pain I felt over my entire body and jerked up. A blinding ache filled my head immediately, but I paid no attention to it.

My eyes flew around me first, looking for the familiar cages...hopefully looking for the familiar faces of Od, Jullian and the rest. I couldn't see anyone nearby, but my ears had begun to catch on the voices of humans...of men. They were getting closer too and my heart had begun to beat faster in my chest. In the split second, I thought about running again but I felt exhausted and thirsty. I wouldn't last three seconds on my feet before I fell back to the ground.

So, I chose to lie back on the blankets and pretended as if I was still unconscious. It took almost forever before the approaching voices felt so near, I could conclude that the men were beside me already. I was anxious. They were no longer speaking. It was as if the men stood and stared down at me, confused. Eventually, I heard a few whispers and then a soft thud as if one of the men was climbing onto the carriage that I slept on.

"We know you are awake already, child."

My eyes fluttered open immediately. I couldn't help it, partly because I was anxious and curious about how they had figured out my pretense.

"We saw you sitting up from afar. It is why I have come with a cup of water while my partner has brought some food."

I was wrong. I hadn't heard the voices of men but rather, the voices of a man and woman. The woman was the one that climbed the carriage to sit only a few inches from me. She had brown skin and long black hair that she tied to the back into a ribbon. Her smile also looked friendly and genuine, making her look oddly beautiful, despite the faint wrinkles beside her eyes and on her forehead.

"Drink." She said, passing over the cup in her hand to me.

I didn't have a choice. I would care about my safety later, I told myself. I was extremely thirsty and lightheaded; so, I downed the entire liquid down my throat immediately when the cup was in my hand. I then passed the cup back to her and blinked twice, expecting her to know that I needed more.

The woman chuckled. She glanced back at her partner who I finally found time to observe. He was a bit taller than her and had a full beard that hid almost half of his face. He glanced at me briefly and scornfully, passed the food in his hands to his partner and left with the cup to get me more water.

"You shouldn't mind him, little one." His partner said to me as soon as he left. "He is always like that to everyone." She said.

I hadn't found my voice, but my mind was back to normal now. I only nodded my head at her, various images of the previous night already filling my head. Where was I? Where are Od and the sisters that had escaped with us? What about Jullian and the others that had stayed back? Was I back with the gang that had kidnapped us? Wasn't I supposed to be dead after I was shot?

The last question almost made me choke. My hands flew to my body immediately, checking for wounds as the imagination of gunshots filled my mind.

"You are okay. You are safe. Whatever happened to you, little one?"

Tears welled up in my eyes as the woman in front of me moved closer, knelt in front of me and held my hand. She was only trying to console me, but the result was a pool of water running down my cheeks. I couldn't control the sadness creeping into my heart. I still felt fear too since I was aware that whatever new place I was, it wasn't the town Od had spoken of.

"Where am I, please?" I finally muttered, hating the coarse child-like whisper of my voice.

"The outskirt of Noyon."

"Noyon?" I asked, seemingly lost.

35

"Yes." I was told. "We are in Southern Mongolia, dear. Noyon is one of the districts of the Omnogovi Province here."

Oh Mongolia, I thought. I was still home. Thinking about it a second time though, my eyes trailing the edges of the barren land that surrounded where we were, I knew I wasn't home. I was far away from home. Omnogovi Province; Noyon, I had never heard of either of them before.

"How did I get here, uh...?"

"Tuya." The woman provided when she noticed I was having a problem with addressing her. "You can call me Tuya and my partner, who is already coming with a full jug of water for you, by the way, is Xanadu."

Xanadu arrived just in time and passed the jug to me, along with the food he had left earlier which Tuya had dropped beside her when she moved closer to console me.

"She should eat and drink," Xanadu said. "She looks like she had been through a lot."

They were kind; I had to acknowledge that. Tuya had also mentioned it earlier that I was safe, and I felt the urge to believe her. Staring at both, I finally dug my hand into the food and took my first bite along with a new gulp of water.

"Regarding your previous question," I heard Tuya mutter, "we found you this morning underneath a heavy heap of sands. You were completely covered above except for your fingers. When we dug you out, you were slightly breathing and only had a few bruises on your legs and the sides of your head. We thought you couldn't be the only one since we assumed you were traveling and involved in an accident or...."

"I wasn't." I interrupted, still hate my voice. It used to be better and happier.

"Oh," Tuya said. "What happened then?"

I was rushing the food down my throat and seldom had a chance to breathe or talk. It took a few seconds before I could stop chewing and decide to tell both Tuya and Xanadu how I had been kidnapped in front of my home and thrown into a cage to be sold off. When I was through recounting my escape, I noticed the ensuing silence that took over the carriage. It was as if both had expected an entirely different tale.

"Where are the men now?" Xanadu asked.

I shook my head, having no care in the world for them. They weren't with me now and that made me happier than the food that I ate did.

"What about home?" Tuya asked. "Do you know where it is?"

Again, I shook my head. Briefly, I let my eyes trail around the vast desert land around me and towards the traces of grassland that surrounded it and then shook my head again.

"You are lost then and have nowhere to go?" Tuya asked again.

This time around, I nodded. I paused and downed a few gulps of water from the jug, noticing the exchange of confused glances between Tuya and Xanadu.

"It's okay then." Tuya finally said. "You have nothing to worry. You finish your food and join us on our journey."

Whatever the concluding clause of her last sentence meant, I wasn't sure I understood it. But I didn't worry much about what I wanted now. I was just glad I was safe and wouldn't die of thirst or hunger.

Tuya patted my feet and slowly dropped from the carriage. It was while she did that I noticed for the first time that the carriage was fixed to two horses like a cart. Someone obviously rode the horses and there were barrels on the carriage as well, probably filled to the brim with oil or coal.

Having no reason to be wary of what I saw, I went back to the rest of my food and ate it quietly. When Xanadu and Tuya noticed that I wasn't saying anything else, they left me alone and walked away, whispering to each other.

"Wait!" I suddenly groaned, remembering what Tuya had said earlier.

"Yes, little one." Tuya stopped walking and turned to face me.

"You said you thought I couldn't be the only one when you found me," I said. "Did you search around for anyone else?"

"No," Tuya whispered. "We spent minutes seeing if we could find anyone you might be traveling with. We found no one."

It felt as if a dagger had been dug into my heart. I nodded, watching as Tuya and Xanadu turned and left me alone finally. Od, Altantsetseg, Chinua, and Khulan were probably caught or worse, dead, I thought. I never knew what really happened to them till date.

I had been lucky. I had the desert sands to thank. My captors probably couldn't find me because of the darkness at the time and because I was buried beneath sands. I meant nothing to them. They probably thought I was going to die lonely without water or food.

I was alive nonetheless. I had been found.

My fate was still undetermined, but I had a glint of hope. A smile plastered across my face just when I realized that Tuya and Xanadu hadn't even asked for my name.

✷✷✷✷✷

Tuya and Xanadu weren't traveling alone.

They came back to the carriage ten minutes later, Tuya asking if I needed more food or water. When I told her I was okay, she smiled and urged me out of the carriage. She then placed her arm over my shoulder and told me I would be having girls like me become my sisters soon.

"We are all traveling together." She told me. "All twelve of us. Some of the girls are just like you. You will like them once you meet them."

I had an odd feeling wash over me when Tuya said that the girls were like me twice. I wanted to ask if they were found underneath a heap of sand like I was, or if they were lost children, without any iota of an idea how to return to their families.

I didn't mention either of this to Tuya though. I kept them to myself as I always did and only nodded my head to show my interest in meeting the other children. The sun was rising to the middle of the sky already, indicating that it was afternoon. The breeze and atmosphere were hot and the sweat running down my skin reminded me that I hadn't had a bath since I was taken away from my home.

Eventually, after walking around the carriage, Tuya guided me towards a large boulder where I was astonished to find eleven other people as Tuya had counted, sitting in circles. I hadn't thought she was lying but I hadn't expected that apart from Xanadu and another man who were middle-aged men, the rest of the group would be young girls between the ages of seven and ten.

Everyone glanced up to stare at me as Tuya and I approached them. Xanadu and the other middle-aged man stood briefly and sat back when Tuya urged them to with a wave. She seemed to be the one in charge. The girls oddly cower before her and fixed their gazes to the floor. Once again, I felt Tuya's arm on my shoulder as she addressed everyone.

"Little one, meet the girls." She said. "Everyone, meet...."

"Yuna," I said, wondering for the umpteenth time why she hadn't asked for my name the entire time.

"Yes. Yuna." Tuya iterated. "She will be joining us the rest of the journey."

"Welcome, Yuna." I heard some of the girl's whispers.

"You will get to know each person as soon as you mix with them." Tuya giggled beside me.

I was already busy with my own assessment of each girl. Three of the girls wore gowns with tattered hems as if they had been in a far worse hell than I had been. Or perhaps the clothes were given to them instead of being thrown away as an act of kindness, I corrected myself. These three kept their gaze to the ground, the soft breeze plastering their black hair to the sides of their faces. I concluded at the time that like me, they probably have a story or two to tell.

Four out of the other five girls should be older than I was. They were a bit bolder and kept their gaze between a stare at the ground and a long glance at me and Tuya. If I guessed correctly, they didn't like Tuya one bit or perhaps it was my inclusion in the group that displeased them.

The last girl I noticed looked as young as I was. She was slender, petite and had a smile fixed on her face. I felt some sort of happiness smiling back at her. In all honesty, she made me think of Saran. They both had that distinct cheerfulness on their faces which made them loveable, no matter how demanding or irritable they could be.

Eventually, forming an opinion about each girl within split seconds, I let Tuya lead me towards Xanadu and the other man.

"You know Xanadu already," Tuya said. "Meet his brother, Hulagu."

Hulagu was burly and taller than Xanadu. He had a sterner face and only nodded when I smiled anxiously at him.

"The truck would be here anytime," Hulagu said, his attention fixed on only Tuya.

"Good". Tuya said. "I guess we all have to start preparing for the rest of the journey....at least, with better means of transportation."

I let my gaze go over my shoulder to the horses that had their entire body fixed to the carriage. It was indeed a terrible means of transportation.

"Where are we going from here in a truck?" I asked when I turned back to stare at all three of them – Tuya, Xanadu and Hulagu.

"Chang Rai." Tuya gritted her teeth. "Chang Rai Thailand."

CHAPTER THREE

Chiang Rai

The truck that drove us to Chiang Rai came thirty minutes after I was introduced to the other girls. It had a rusty grey color and its engine sounded like it had worked far better, decades ago. There was only a man in it – the driver – and he seemed to be very familiar with Tuya and her group. Immediately he parked the car close to the cart and switched off the engine, he stepped down, waved curtly at Tuya and pointed to the barrels in the cart.

"How many?" he asked.

"Twelve," Tuya replied.

The driver didn't seem pleased. He stared at the cart as if he was counting the barrels in his head and frowned. "Not exactly what he expects." He hissed.

"Well, you can tell Chuluun that as usual, sometimes, he gets more and sometimes, less." Tuya hissed back.

The driver opened his mouth to say something but seemed to think twice about it. After hissing again, his eyes left the cart and turned to us.

"You picked up strays again?" He asked. "How many this time? Same number as the barrels? By the end of the year, how many would still be...."

"You watch your mouth." Tuya groaned, giving him a freezing glare.

The driver let his eyes linger for a long time on all ten of us before he hissed for the umpteenth time and pointed to his truck.

"Get them all in then; the barrel first. It's going to be a long journey after all and the earlier we start, the earlier we leave this shit hole of a desert."

Their odd discussion seemed to end abruptly at that moment. Tuya nodded at Xanadu and Hulagu who quickly rushed to the cart and began to move the barrels.

"Chop chop!" The driver urged.

It took less than five minutes for the barrel to be fully loaded. Eventually, Tuya turned to us and asked us to climb atop the truck and squeeze ourselves in with the barrels.

"It is the only means of transportation we have got." She muttered kindly. "We will soon get home where you all will get to have a normal life back. You can find your way back home too."

The fact that Tuya spoke nicely and mentioned the possibility of living a happy life (or returning home) made lots of us eager to jump into the truck. We naturally trusted her and despite the weird business going on with the barrels, I also got into the truck with the girls and settled beside the girl that had smiled at me earlier.

"Hi." She whispered, smiling at me once again.

"Hi," I whispered back, a genuine smile plastered on my face.

We said nothing else, our gazes settling on Xanadu and Hulagu who checked to see that the iron fastening of the truck doors was in place.

"All done," Hulagu told Tuya.

"Oh good. Now we go." The driver said beside her.

"Not so fast," Tuya said.

She made a facial gesture that got Xanadu and Hulagu to step away with her immediately. They spoke in hushed tones and a few seconds later, it seemed as if an argument had broken out. Hulagu kept pointing to the truck. He shook his head too and seldom pointed to his brother, Xanadu. Eventually, Tuya groaned at each man and silenced them. We all could only watch from the truck as Hulagu eventually nodded and began to walk towards the cart.

"Now, we go," Tuya said, walking back towards the truck with only Xanadu.

"What about the other man? Isn't he coming with us?" I expected someone to ask, but no one did. The driver simply hurried into the truck, Tuya, and Xanadu settling beside him, and roared the engine alive.

"Get this thing on the road fast." I heard Tuya say as the truck began a slow drive down the desert road. "I want nothing more than a hot bath as soon as I get to Chiang Rai."

We all do, I thought to myself.

✳✳✳✳✳

Chiang Rai was a capital city in the Chiang Rai Province in Thailand. It was a large city that had caves, lots of Buddhist temples, streets with free cultural performances and display of crafts, and countless restaurants.

At least, these were the few things that I noticed about the city as we drove in. We had been on the road nonstop for two days. The only time we ever stopped was for a gas refill for the truck and for us to ease ourselves. Tuya passed food for us to share amidst ourselves during each time that the truck stopped. She also got us water from the gas station and told us to manage whatever we have got since the journey was still long.

While we kept moving, passing along various hills, more desert land, and grasslands, I finally got to know the names of a few of the girls. The girl that had smiled at me earlier told me her name was Cyril. Her Mongolian father had married a European woman who had died at childbirth. In his wife's memory, he had given her name to their daughter. Cyril spoke little English and stuttered a little. She was slim and beautiful too. I couldn't help but notice her good set of teeth, hazel eyes, long eyelashes, and wavy black hair.

There was also Taban, Qara and Sarnai. They were the three girls I had noticed earlier with worn out dresses. Cyril had told me about them in hushed tones, expressing how weird she felt with the way they stared at the floor all the time. According to her, it meant that they had something to hide and I had a tough time convincing her that it meant that they were afraid or shy instead.

"Those you should be more concerned about are those four," I told her, referring to the rest of the girls who seemed older than the rest of us. Two of them stared briefly at us and nudged their noses rudely.

"Them?" Cyril had asked, seeming surprised.

"Yes." I insisted. "They stare all the time and seem not to like me."

I had to refrain from mentioning that they didn't look like they liked Tuya too. I appreciated that I held that back though, especially when Cyril sighed and explained that the older girls had been with Tuya more than the rest of us had.

"Tuya found me close to where you were found," Cyril told me. "She had been traveling almost six days with them before then. She promised that she was going to take them somewhere safe and take care of them. I think they adore her instead."

I wanted to argue but Cyril quickly added, "What they don't like would be us- the rest of us that were found after they were. We reduce the chance of them ever getting everything they were promised."

I thought about the truth in Cyril's words the rest of the journey. What I also thought about was how odd that we were all girls. Didn't Tuya come across any male child to rescue? What was the real possibility that everyone was found coincidentally? Could Tuya really offer everything she promised each one of us?

Each time I thought about discussing this with Cyril, I got discouraged, especially since I suspect that Cyril adored Tuya too. I was also uncertain that I wasn't just afraid because of everything I had been through. I still couldn't sleep without having nightmares. I always fell deep into a dark hole in them. Sometimes, I had flashes of images – of Mother and Father becoming old, fragile and sad because I was gone forever.

Whenever I woke up, Cyril would be beside me, her fingers clutching mine. She had nightmares too. I had heard her groan in the middle of the night too and had to snuggle close to her, so we could cuddle and lay still. Eventually, we learned to hold hands whenever we were concerned about anything and didn't want to talk about it.

After two days of riding through harsh sunny weather during the day and freezing cold during the night, we eventually arrived at Chiang Rai. The city was bordered by ranges in the north and another one in the south. We drove over a large river before heading into the town – the scene before us already exciting a few of us.

We noticed the busy lifestyle, the trade on the streets and the way children played at the entrances of various temples. Instead of stopping within the city though, the truck kept moving until we were at another part of the city with fewer houses, a few hills, and vast plain lands.

"We are stopping," Cyril whispered, having been anxious since the moment we arrived in the city.

The truck did stop. Glancing around, I noticed that we were on a land like the steep my parents and I lived in Mongolia. It was quiet, compared to the buzzing city center we had left behind. There weren't many houses around too and the house in front of the truck was an old-looking shed with tinted window glasses, wooden pillars, and a small porch.

Xanadu stepped out of the truck to help us with the iron doors. While we hurried down, Tuya spoke with the driver quietly and didn't attend to us until she was done. The driver nodded curtly, stepped into the truck and drove off, faster than we arrived. He left with the barrels too.

"Here." Tuya persuaded us towards the house as the truck raced into the city center. "The house is a small one but there are five rooms, enough to house you all."

She explained as we stepped onto the porch. "Xanadu will show you all to the rooms while I get some things sorted out somewhere else."

"What about my parents, Tuya?" One of the older girls suddenly asked as Tuya made a move to step away from us.

"Oh, but you have only been here a few minutes." Tuya grinned. "We will find them as soon as possible. They should be in the city as I have told you earlier."

The older girl nodded and managed to smile briefly. Whatever agreement she had had with Tuya, she had expected that it would be carried out immediately when she got to Chiang Rai. It didn't seem like it would happen anytime soon either. The part about her parents being in the city also confused me.

Tuya left us alone eventually, Xanadu leading us into the house. The house was empty except for a few chairs and table which seemed dusty as if they hadn't been used in weeks. We were led towards the small hall with the four rooms.

"Four in a room," Xanadu instructed. "Tuya stays in the first room while the rest are for customers."

Immediately, the girls began to divide themselves into groups while I singly wondered about the word *customers*. Perhaps people came around for the oil barrels, I told myself. I didn't have time to think much. A few seconds later, I noticed everyone else was staring at me.

"You would have to make it five in a room then. Tuya wasn't planning for a ninth girl I think." Xanadu said when I stared back at him questioningly.

It took me a second to realize that the girls were now in a set of two. The four older girls had chosen to stay together while Cyril, Taban, Qara, and Sarnai had also hurdled together as a group.

"Well?" Xanadu asked as if he had asked a question earlier.

"She will join us." I heard Cyril say.

Short of words and still finding everything disorienting, I nodded and stepped towards the group

Luke. G. Dahl

of girls I had come to know a little throughout the journey. Cyril smiled at me and held my hand.

"Into the rooms," Xanadu told us all, both hands pointing to doors at opposite sides of the hall. "Water would be prepared soon for your refreshment. There are new clothes in the rooms too. You all need to be all washed up and dressed before nightfall. Tuya would be back then with friends."

Friends. Friends.

Something was off, I kept telling myself. I couldn't pinpoint what it was, but I could sense danger in my gut. In the past week that I had been taken from the home, I had escaped from my own captors. I had grown. I could sense danger now, but all were the same with how I could prevent them.

It was worse now anyway. I was an eight-year-old child; an expatriate without a single idea about the city I had found myself and the path that led back to the home I left behind.

All five of us stepped into our room for the first time, welcoming the arid smell of decay and slaving future.

We totally didn't expect that our lives were about to take a new drastic turn.

CHAPTER FOUR

Broken

...Sixteen Months Later

The room was quiet and dark. It had been specially built with two small windows that had strong iron bars and tinted glasses to keep the sun out as well as make it impossible for anyone to see what was going on inside.

I didn't know what day it was. I hardly do anymore. I could only feel few rays of the sun stubbornly slithering into the room and lighting up everywhere with dim bright colors. No lamp was lit. None had ever been. Electricity only went as far as the passage and the sitting room. The room I was in was usually used by two clients, who were usually very particular about dark rooms and hiding their identities.

I wasn't anxious. It wasn't my first time either ever since my arrival in Chiang Rai. With the beauty of the large city came sadness for the girls and me, and half of us had already accepted our fates. We had begun to live our lives as the decadent young girls we have been made to become.

As I lay on the bed, nothing else crossed my mind except for the expectation that my client would come in, defile me as he did once in a week, wipe himself afterward and leave me to sob all alone.

He slid in through the door eventually, his burly figure always being the significant thing about him. He smelled of a fresh shave and breathed like he smoked all the time. There was a loud click as he locked the door behind him, groaned like a famished animal and began to step towards me.

"Are you ready for me today as always, little one?" his croaky voice resounded through the room walls.

He asked the same question all the time as if my opinion mattered. The first time he was with me and I had tried to resist him, we had ended the session with half of my chest stained with my own blood. I had nursed a broken lip and swollen eyes for weeks and no one had offered to help. The other girls had problems of their own to solve.

"How about we try something different today, uh?" He was asking me now.

I hadn't noticed that my gaze had glued to the ceiling as soon as he stepped into the room. I stared at him now, noticing a small shiny object in his hand. He was flinging it around as if to prepare me for whatever he could do to me with it.

"What is it?" I asked, my voice almost failing me.

I didn't have that girl-like voice anymore. In fact, I had no voice. It was only a faint whisper; one that had become a part of me ever since the innocent and free girl in me had been ripped off.

"Hell, I don't even know what it is." I heard him laugh. "You are supposed to drink half of it and feel so good while we are at it."

He slid towards me on the bed, his fingers already trailing the edges of my slender legs. I knew what the object in his hand was now. It was a small bottle with a very familiar blue liquid. New girls in the shed were made to drink it the first time a man was to be with them. It slowed down their senses and weakened them, making it impossible for them to know what was happening until rods were deep in their thighs and they were bleeding out with pain.

For the girls who had been through that stage already – as I have – drinking the blue liquid only made it impossible to go through the formidable activity of sex – without remorse, without restraint to not enjoy every part of it.

"So, are you going to drink it, little one?"

Little One, I thought with a sad smile. The name had stuck for the past two years. It was the name Tuya called me. It was also the name she had adopted whenever she introduced me to the men. Those that had forced their horrid dicks into the hole between my thighs also muttered the name whenever they needed me to do something that they liked...or whenever they were near the end of their lust.

Tonight, it was about getting high on a drug and doing horrible things I might not like.

I didn't tell him though. I couldn't. I wasn't allowed to say anything I wasn't asked or told to say. So, I just opened my mouth instead, indicating that he could feed me the opium. The liquid burnt my throat as usual before settling down in my already-anxious body and getting the entire hair on it erect.

"Well, you took it all instead of half." I heard him giggle. "Today is really about doing something different."

I only nodded, fear already creeping into my heart. I could feel my small breasts growing hard. My nipples hardened too while every inch of my body began to feel a drop of sweat.

"It is already working, isn't it?" I heard him ask.

I nodded quickly, having no complaint in the world as his hands gripped my dress and tore it off me with a single yank. I was naked underneath. We always were. His strong palm gripped my throat afterward while his other hand went to one of my breasts. He gripped tightly, squeezing remorselessly.

"Beautiful, little one." He said. "They are just beautiful...your breasts."

He bit on them hard while he groaned happily. He squeezed my throat too, seeming pleased every time that I choked. I was in-between mouth intake of breath when he suddenly knelt beside me and jerked his manhood into my mouth.

Somehow, despite how nauseated I ought to feel, it felt like a relief having his rod deep inside my mouth instead of his palm around my neck. I did what he wanted. I choked on it first before biting softly and suckling at the same time. It was big, but I managed to push half of it deep into my mouth without hurting myself.

"Take it all in." I heard him say. "Swallow everything."

I did. I don't know how or what urged me on, but I did. I reached up, knelt and closed my palms around the end of his rod. I jerked back and forth, pulling out and pushing in his manhood through my lips until nothing else was out to grip.

"It really worked magic uh, the liquid. You have never been this mild."

He was laughing at my obedience. They always did, despite that, we had no choice than to be obedient.

He was shedding off every bit of esteem I had left, and I could only do everything he wanted. It was how it ended soon. There was no use fighting it. I had tried to. We all had at one point in the past two years and we always get back to the point where we must be raped by more than one man.

"Well, I think it is high time we get to real business, little one. You only have to lay still. I won't hurt you."

He always said this before the pain began. They all did. It was usually that moment before my frail fragile body would be laid on the bed while my thighs are spread apart for easy penetration. It hurt all the time.

"Good girl. There. Just lie there."

He was aggressively pushing me toward the center of the bed. I tried to see the expression on his face, but I could make out nothing except for his pointed nose and short hair. He was huge too, his wide shoulders seeming like a shadow that was about to devour me whole.

"Please." I managed to whisper.

It was too late. It always was. He knelt in front of me, spread my thighs wide and forced it in, the pain was indescribable. Everything became blurry afterward as groans filled the entire room. It was always their groans against our silence.

It was late in the evening by the time I stepped out of the room, my torn dress clutched to my chest. I could see the descending sun as well as the rays of orange light through the small window at the end of the passage. With sadness always creeping in my heart nowadays, I ignored the urge to admire both and slowly began the stride towards the resting room instead.

Resting room. It was the name we had to give to the two rooms where we all slept. This was because Tuya or Xanadu always barked at us to head to the rooms and rest before another client arrived and needed our service.

There shouldn't be a reason to mince words. Tuya had gotten us through hell just to land us in another one. We were her whores now. The promises of finding a safe place for us were all lies. We were never going to be united with our families. We were goods to Tuya – some sort of objects that could be used and reused by the men that patronized her little whorehouse.

Tuya had been strategic with the location of the house. It had been built at the edge of the city to keep activities around us minimal as well as make it feel like a safe haven to her clients instead. Local authorities came around sometimes and they either asked for money or asked to go a few rounds with the girls. We had once thought they could save us but that was in the past now. Any shred of hope was in the past now.

When I got into the restroom, I deliberately dropped my dress to the floor and heaved a long sigh. The room was dark and empty. It wasn't my excuse anyway. I was just exhausted. My entire body hurts. At the top of all these was the tears that began to rush down my cheeks as I thought about how over ten men had slept with me in the span of just four days. Despite all the drugs, I didn't enjoy any of them. Some of the men slapped me. Most of them pushed their heavyweight atop of me, making it impossible to breathe...to exist.

"Yuna?"

Someone was in the room with me. I suddenly noticed a slow movement at the end of the room. Wincing, I stepped towards the bed there and bit my lips, realizing who it was.

"Cyril," I said. "Are you okay?"

Cyril shook her head. She was crying too. The straps of her dress hung down her shoulders while her entire back dripped of sweat.

"What is wrong?" I asked her.

"Everything," Cyril whispered, her voice rising into a wail. "Everything!" She repeated. "I will never be okay with everything."

I understood what she meant. I felt the same thing, although I felt that I was doing better than she was. Cyril had always been the most emotional one amongst us. She still felt traumatized ever since her first rape. Her nightmares were constant now. She screamed every night and sometimes told me that she had the urges to end her own life.

"Just a few more years," I told Cyril. "Tuya promised us we would only have to work here seven years and she would give us freedom."

"Freedom," Cyril said, her voice seemingly distant. "You speak as if it would ever feel as it should feel after everything we have done.... after everything that has been done to us."

I didn't have the answers that Cyril wanted. Lost for words, I only stepped towards her and held her hand. I sat on the bed and pulled her towards me, so she could sit and lay her head on my lap. I began to play with her hair then, the room echoing with her sobs. She had long since cut her hair in half, stating that it made her feel – as she should feel – less than the girl she once was.

I remember the first few days we had both been in the restroom, excited about Chiang Rai. Tuya had returned the first evening with two men and had introduced them as caretakers. She had made us look good first before arranging us in a single line in front of them. They came into the restroom, grinning like hungry wolves. Eventually, both men had nodded as if they were pleased with what they had seen and had left the room for the next one.

That night, two of the older girls didn't eat dinner with us. We could hear loud groans and faint whispers in the other rooms but Tuya had told us that it was nothing. She told us not to ever be afraid and we believed her. Eventually, four nights later, late in the night, strong arms had come for us, dragging us into the other rooms.

I could remember how loud I screamed, thinking it was one of my few nightmares. I thought I was being kidnapped again but the thought ended when I was dragged to the passage and standing in front of me was Tuya. She smirked briefly at me and nodded at the men behind me. They turned out to be Hulagu, Xanadu and a few other men I hadn't seen before. I wasn't even aware Hulagu had returned from the desert days before.

"She is ready," Tuya told the men, pointing to me. "She can be a hellcat too, so do not take any chances with her."

The same things were said of Cyril too. We were both dragged off in different directions afterward, and then our clothes were torn off promptly before our bodies were pulled into dark rooms. I cried throughout the whole night. I couldn't move around the house myself for a while. My muscles hurt. I felt lightheaded all the time.

"Do you remember them at all?" It took me a second before I could jolt my mind back to the present. Cyril had asked a question. I thought she was falling asleep but apparently, she was lost in thoughts as well.

"Remember them?" I inquired.

"Your parents," Cyril whispered. "It's only been two years and I can no longer remember mine. I only remember that Clifford bakes good cakes every Friday."

"Clifford? Was that your father's name?" I whispered.

"No," Cyril said. "He comes around to look after me whenever Dad wasn't around."

I nodded, my mind temporarily drifting off to the delicious food that Mother cooked too. There was no way I could remember the precise taste but there was no avoiding the image of how excited I was whenever she did the cooking.

"So, do you remember their faces?" Cyril asked again.

I didn't know what to say. I thought I would but the imagination of Father's seldom smile was no longer profound in my head. Saran would be older now, I thought. I couldn't even remember the sound of her laughter or Mother's smile as she watched us play.

"I don't think I do." I finally told Cyril.

There was absolute silence afterward. Cyril heaved a long sigh and slept, her fingers still clutching mine while my other hand caressed her hair. I closed my eyes too, knowing full well it wasn't the end of the day yet.

We only had a few minutes of solitude to ourselves. If we were lucky, we would go the rest of the night without having any man force himself into us anymore.

But we have never been lucky ever since we were taken from our home.

CHAPTER FIVE

Peak Season

Once in a month, the girls and I always had to listen to Tuya talk about how ungrateful we were that she had taken us in instead of allowing us to rot in the middle of the desert. This usually happened during a monthly meeting that she set up to always remind us that we were only to work for her for seven years, and then become independent to do whatever we wanted with our lives.

She always complained about the same thing – how the older girls had learned to satisfy her clients while Cyril, Taban, Qara, Sarnai and I were always so childish and frigid. Cyril usually got rebuked because she was always crying whenever the men were with her. Some of them had complained that this turned their urges off or irritated them. They never told Tuya though that they always had to beat Cyril out of irritation or just forcibly penetrate her thighs.

Tuya was furious when she called for us at the end of another month, her eyes burning with irritation. She pointed at Cyril a few times as she spoke and sometimes hit a fist on the table. Eventually, she stopped talking and glared at every single one of us.

"And some of you also had the guts to attempt to run away!" She spat.

Run away? I thought with a frown then. *Why haven't I ever thought of that? Why haven't I thought of stepping away from the borders of the house and get lost within the city? It was a big one after all.*

"Sarnai? Qara? You girls have anything to say?"

Tuya obviously was demanding for an explanation. Cyril and I shared a confused look as both girls stepped forward and knelt in front of a still-furious Tuya.

"We weren't trying to run away," Qara said. "Sarnai and I were only trying to see the city."

"We have been locked in the house for so long, Tuya," Sarnai added. "We just thought we could go out a while and come back before...."

Sarnai couldn't complete her last sentence. Tuya's palm landed hard on her face, shutting her up and rendering the rest of us silent and shocked at the same time.

"I am not a fool, you idiots," Tuya shouted. "You packed your bags – everything I bought for you – and tried to board a ship yesterday afternoon. Xanadu here saw you leaving the house while Hulagu had your ship pass with him all the time. Do you think you would do anything in this city or have any of my clients help you to escape and Tuya would know nothing about it?"

The situation was obvious now. Sarnai and Qara had obviously trusted someone – one of the men that raped, beaten or tortured them – to help them escape. It had only been a set up as Tuya had known about it all and had found them before they could set sail and escape.

"We are sorry." Qara was crying now. She was shivering as her arms stretched forward to grip Tuya's feet.

"Oh, but you aren't worry yet." Tuya hissed. "You will be soon."

She waved her hands and Xanadu and Hulagu stepped forward immediately. They threw both Qara and Sarnai over their shoulders and left the sitting room, both girls wailing so loud the entire house still echoed with their cries long after we could hear them no more.

"Perhaps you all could learn from what happened today," Tuya groaned, turning to the rest of us. "I have always been kind. I helped you. I gave you a home...."

I was no longer listening. I had thought about the reason I hadn't thought about my own escape before. I know now – it was because I had been in the position before. They always caught up with us – our kidnappers or masters. I would have been back in the syndicate cart I escaped from years ago if the desert sands had not been kind to me. If I left now, the same way Qara and Sarnai had attempted to, it would only take such little effort to find me.

"What will happen to them?"

The words had blurted out of my mouth before I could control myself. My curiosity had driven towards whatever would be done to Qara and Sarnai.

"Them? Oh, do you mean your friends who decided to trash my kindness?"

"Yes," I said, nodding my head. I hadn't expected a response or her calmness towards me.

"What would happen to them?" I asked again.

"Nothing damaging, I promise. Let's just say it is the peak season and both would be needed somewhere else."

I became silent. I didn't understand a single thing that she had said. Nonetheless, I nodded and bit my lips, having a feeling that things were about to become worse for Qara and Sarnai, and as usual, there was nothing any of us could do about it.

"Now, how about new instructions for the house?" Tuya muttered a second later, stepping towards the center of the sitting room. "Henceforth," she said, "every girl is to have no conversation with the men. You are to do everything they say, clean up afterward and wait for further instructions. I know some of you think you have grown up already and old enough to contact the authorities. No one will help you but Tuya, you hear. I have helped you thus far; don't ever forget that."

There were a few more instructions about how we should walk, speak and act with each man that visited the house and we all pretended to listen attentively – or perhaps I was the only one that did.

Eventually, when the talk was over, Tuya announced that she would be leaving for a few days while Xanadu and Hulagu would be back to take care of everyone. She dismissed the meeting and was about to head for the door when Hulagu came in through the door and whispered in her ear. Tuya nodded and pointed to us.

"They are not to step foot out of the house for the two to three days I am gone." She groaned.

Hulagu shrugged his broad shoulders and gave his usual curt frown. As soon as Tuya was gone, he turned to us with the same frown and had us hurrying towards the restrooms without a single word. Cyril held on to my hand as we moved. It felt as if she was terrified suddenly. She kept staring into my eyes, pleading for something I couldn't figure out in an instant. I thought about asking her what was wrong but suddenly, Hulagu was behind us with his eyes fixated on Cyril's chest.

"You stay behind." He grinned, pointing to Cyril.

"Why, Master Hulagu?" Cyril asked with a trembling voice. She clutched my fingers tighter, almost breaking them.

"Oh well, you are not to ask questions. It doesn't matter anyway; even Yuna can watch."

Watch what! I was appalled. Staring at both Cyril and Hulagu, I suddenly realized that Hulagu had been one of the men constantly raping Cyril. Neither of them mentioned it but Hulagu's palm had suddenly gripped Cyril's breast while his cheeks rose up in absolute admiration and lust.

"We can do what we did the last time, uh, sweetie?" He said as if I wasn't even there to see him behave like a psychopathic pervert.

"Leave her alone." I tried to whisper but my voice always failed me when I needed it. My words came out as a soft breath instead of a groan.

I could only watch as Hulagu dragged Cyril towards him. We were still at the passage and everyone else seemed to have disappeared in a jiffy. Cyril dragged me with her and whatever Hulagu did to her, I had to watch, dumbstruck.

Tears rushed down Cyril's cheeks already. Hulagu gave me a freezing stare before reaching down underneath Cyril's dress. Cyril tried to clasp her thighs together to resist him but Hulagu reached forward with his second hand to strike her across the face. When I impulsively stepped forward, the same hand hit my cheek, keeping me rooted to where I was.

"You just watch," Hulagu told me. "You don't have to move."

Hulagu had become aggressive. The next time he reached for Cyril, he raised her off her feet, severing the clutch of our fingers. He held her throat next and pulled up her dress, so it could hang around her neck. His lips closed around her left nipple next while his other hand was already feeling the edges of her thighs.

I looked around helplessly now, thinking about how to put a stop to what was happening. There was nothing I could do. I was always helpless. I felt so useless. I was never trained to be an adult at an so early age. I never had to take care of anyone, or myself.

"What the hell are you doing? Tuya only just left you fool!"

There was a fourth person in the passage suddenly. I felt relieved for the first time to set my eyes on Xanadu. Hulagu stepped back from Cyril abruptly, though he still kept his palm around her neck. Xanadu's eyes moved from Hulagu to the roughened texture of Cyril's dress and then to the helplessness that was visible on my face.

"Walk away, Xanadu." Hulagu hissed. "This doesn't concern you."

"Oh, but it does," Xanadu said, shaking his head and taking further steps towards us. "Unless you would prefer that I put in a word about this to Tuya when she gets back."

"Then what, you idiot?" Hulagu asked, already cursing under his breath.

Xanadu hadn't expected that Hulagu would be defiant and unrepentant. He was speechless for a few seconds before he pointed to Cyril and began to stammer like a man who was unsure of every word that left his lips.

"That...that...you are the reason the poor...poor girl hasn't been strong enough to face any of the men and...and pleasure them. You break each one more than they already are, you fool."

Xanadu's speech influenced Hulagu eventually. He groaned, stepped away from Cyril finally and spat at our feet. Cyril ran into my arms immediately, sobbing uncontrollably. I felt sad about everything. I felt sadder that I hadn't known what to do. I just stood there as I always did whenever each of us was defiled.

At that moment, anger sieving through my bones, I silently promised myself that I would find a way to be stronger. I needed to be able to do something whenever I was being hurt, or whenever those that I loved were in pain.

Hulagu strode off, saying nothing to us, or to Xanadu. Xanadu stayed behind though and took a step towards us. We stepped backward impulsively, suddenly afraid of him too. We had to fear every man now. The home we lived in wasn't a safe haven. It was hell simply because we were girls that could be taken advantage of at any time.

"Go into the restrooms," Xanadu told us with a sigh. It was as if he pitied us – an emotion he often had to dismiss.

"Do not step out until evening." He told us. "And clean up too."

I slowly nudged Cyril towards the door and nodded, thanking Xanadu. His footsteps disappeared down the passage as we stepped into the room. Tarban was the only girl with us now and she hid behind the shelf, obviously aware of what transpired outside the room. Immediately we stepped in, she joined us at the bed and sprawled beside us, sobbing.

The room became utterly quiet and I thought the day would end that way until Tarban cleared her throat and said, "I know what will happen to them."

I didn't need to ask who she spoke about. I just kept quiet and let her talk.

"Qara and Sarnai." She said. "They will be sold off or forced to go somewhere else to work. Bangkok maybe. Rai – he smells of alcohol all the time he has been in the room with me – he said a week ago that he helps to sell some of the girls that had been here before us, especially towards the end of the year."

*Peak seaso*n. I remembered that Tuya had mentioned that earlier. Somehow, I also remembered how long it had taken before she realized that she could do away with us one by one. The promise of independence after seven years didn't seem realistic to me anymore.

That night, I realized that it was going to be exactly four years since Tuya brought us to Chiang Rai.

CHAPTER SIX

Death and Bangkok

It had been another year since that incident with Hulagu.

When Tuya came back, nothing had been said. She came back five days later with four new girls that were at least two years younger than we were. She introduced them to us and instead of the deception cards she had played with us, she immediately got the new girls oriented about their jobs. Six men had come for them that night and the rest of the New Year had gone by with the usual incidents.

Sex. More men. Rape. Drugs. Torture. They became the life we were used to, and the majority of us had learned to live with it. In fact, Cyril didn't cry every night anymore. She didn't talk about her parents or ask about mine, either. What she always spoke about was her hopes to return to Mongolia after her seven years was done and start all over again. I found her sudden nonchalance weird though.

"I would forget about all these." She usually said. "I would bake cakes, just like the one I enjoyed as a child."

I always encouraged her with a smile. We sang songs sometimes, having made up lyrics ourselves all the time that we sobbed in sorrow. I sometimes consider that my life could be all about singing after I became free, but sometimes, I just think it was a dream too big for a girl as broken as I am.

Since things had become normal for us at the shed, neither Cyril nor I were prepared for the incident that happened towards the end of the year. It was late in the night and Xanadu had come to get us. He instructed us quickly that we were to go to the dark rooms and get ready to receive clients. We mutely nodded and dispersed into various rooms, hoping to get everything done with and count the rest of the year as steps towards our freedom.

The room I went to afterward was the usual one men enjoyed having sex with me. I had been in it countless times and sometimes I used to think it was the same one where I had been raped for the first time. I cannot remember the incident precisely – there had been so many after it, it became difficult to say which one came first.

As I lay down on the bed, I could hear thudding sounds in the other room already and I imagined that Cyril was already halfway through with her activity. I wondered if she felt the same pain I felt between my thighs after every sex. It seemed men with bigger rods always chose me whenever they came around. Whatever pleasured them about it, I was yet to figure out.

The thudding sound was getting louder and there were groans too. At a point, I heard Cyril's shriek and I winced, guessing that the client this time around was either too big or was after a BDSM. I was also wondering why anyone wasn't in the room with me too. I closed my eyes though, partially listening to the noise in the next room and expecting that the door to mine would creak open any time soon.

I was asleep before I knew it. I missed a few minutes that had passed quickly. By the time I opened my eyes, there was absolute silence around me while the door creaked open slowly. It took a while for my vision to adjust around the room, so I glanced around horrendously. It was only Cyril though, and I jerked up on the bed, wondering why something seemed so off about her appearance.

"Help me." I heard her whisper. "Help me."

"What are you talking about?" I asked her, already hurrying towards her.

Getting close, my palms flew to my mouth. Cyril was completely naked. At first, I thought her entire body dripped of sweat but on another look, I realized the liquid was red and thick. Blood stained her arms, face, palms, and back. She kept glancing back and forth before eventually staring into my eyes, pleading silently.

"What have you done?" I asked. "What have you done?"

"I couldn't take them both. I couldn't." She whispered.

"Them?" I thought to myself.

Various images were rushing through my head and to calm my already-pacing heart, I hurried out of the room towards the next one. She was supposed to be with one man while the other one came to me. What had happened?

I got my response as soon as I barged into the next room.

Two lifeless bodies were in the room. Everywhere was painted red while liquid flowed on the cemented floor, forming a large pool. Behind me, Cyril stepped into the room, her face glued to the floor while her body shook nervously.

Unable to keep the entire shock to myself, a loud shriek escaped my lips.

"The other man came into the room and glanced at me once with a smile on his face. He joined in then, the first man getting excited instead of irritated. They began to hit me. They hit me everywhere... They jolted a whole fist into my vagin...."

Tears ran down Cyril's cheeks as she narrated her ordeal to everyone. Tuya was in the room now, along with Hulagu and Xanadu. The other girls had tried to peep inside the room but Hulagu had given them a single glance and they had all rushed into the restrooms. The door was locked now, and all five of us stood, listening to Cyril and throwing a few disgusted looks at the blood and lifeless bodies on the floor.

Tuya was furious, despite that she hadn't raised her voice at Cyril yet. Fear was boldly apparent in her eyes. Whoever the men Cyril had killed was, having their lifeless bodies in the room seemed to make her nervous. She paced the room as Cyril spoke, her eyes never leaving the lifeless bodies for more than a second.

"I told them to stop." Cyril kept on with her explanation. "They didn't. Even when I hit the first with the lamp post, the second still thought it was all part of the play. He wanted me to hit him. He begged me to. His fist kept forcing its way between my thighs while I hit him, and he didn't stop until he was dead..."

"So, two men came for you and you think you could just kill them? It isn't the first time, dammit."

Tuya had finally lost it. Her eyes went red with anger and frustration, and if Xanadu had not stepped in between her and Cyril, Tuya could have killed Cyril with her bare hands. She threw those hands into the air instead and let them drop to her waist.

96

"What are my options?" She asked her henchmen.

Hulagu shrugged and pointed to the dead men. "You have a rule about clients that do not follow agreements, Tuya." He said. "They both asked for a single and paid exactly the amount for this. Ending up dead sure suits them since they had settled for a double, against their initial order."

"I just preferred that the death had come from my hands." Tuya sighed.

"We would have to dump, clean the room and make it seem like they killed themselves." Xanadu suddenly chirped in. "Suits them or not, this is bad for business. No one would want to have the kids anymore...."

"Or no one would even want to step into the shed. The police might not cooperate anymore too."

Tuya kept gritting her teeth as all three of them weighed her options to avoid a scandal for her business. It, however, shocked me to notice that none of them was really concerned about how hurt Cyril was. Since no one paid her any attention after her narration, she slowly backed against the wall and closed her eyes, her chest slowly rising and falling.

I picked up a shawl from a nearby hanger and approached her with it. She smiled briefly when I covered her nakedness with it and held my hand, thanking me with a nod.

"Are you okay?" I whispered beside her.

She shook her head and bit her lips as if she was hurting, frightened and confused at the same time.

"Tuya will take care of this," I told her, despite that I now doubted that Tuya cared about taking care of anyone but herself.

Cyril nodded, not because she believed my words too but because she really had no choice but to hope that everything would go away. We both watched as Tuya, Hulagu and Xanadu argued, Xanadu pointing to the bloodstained walls of the room and how everything could be arranged as if one of the men had killed the other because of Cyril. The next story would be that the first man had then tried to kill Cyril who had no choice than to defend herself. Of course, they also considered the option of just doing away with the corpses and everyone keeping quiet about their disappearance.

I held Cyril's hands throughout the entire discussion. I could think of various scenarios now, especially regarding some of us that had disappeared over the years. What if they had been killed, instead of sold, while their bodies have been gotten rid of without trace? What would happen to us if we were ever sold off too?

I hadn't even begun to think of that when I noticed that everyone had turned to stare at Cyril and me.

"We should get them out of the city too." I heard Hulagu groan. "They both know everything."

"Both and not just Cyril?" Tuya whispered.

"Yes. They both know everything." Hulagu iterated.

Why I was tempted to ask. I didn't get a chance to though as I noticed Tuya waving a hand dismissively without even a second thought.

"They will be gone before sunrise then." She said. "Contact Bat Erdene that there will be new intakes for the peak season. He can have them if he wants to."

Despite that I didn't know by her words what "gone" meant, I thought about stepping forward and pleading with her to let us stay while we promised to keep our mouths shut. I didn't get a chance to do this either.

Suddenly, Cyril slumped forward, the shawl I had given to her earlier dropping near a pool of red. She hit the floor with a loud thud while her body subsequently began to shake violently and then became still and lifeless.

"Oh crap!" Tuya groaned.

I couldn't move. All I could think about was how more miserable my life would become if Cyril was gone, forever.

Tuya was never known to be a bluffing woman.

The next morning, Cyril and I were indeed in a truck on its way to Bangkok. I wasn't even sure if the means of transportation had been a moving van or a ship. I was unconscious all through the journey. So was Cyril. We had been heavily drugged the night before and by the time we opened our eyes, it was another night and the shed we lived in was different.

The entire time that I was unconscious, it was as if the moment of my kidnap replayed in my head. Something was different in the memory that I had this time around. I was in front of Father's house as an eight-year-old again while strong arms gripped me from behind and rode me into the sunset. This time around, I noticed that I could see the silhouette of a figure close to Father's house, staring intently as the men took me away. The figure shook his head slowly and despite my effort to catch his attention by screaming, it was as if he didn't care that I was taken. He wanted me gone. Feeling hopeless, I shut my eyes and cried.

I was finally glad when I opened my eyes and realized that the memory was gone. I was on a new bed and the usual rusty smell of the restroom wasn't what radiated around the room. I noticed Cyril becoming conscious beside me and glanced at her with a curious frown. Cyril looked frail by the way. The top of her head was bruised while her once-beautiful and lush-looking upper lip seemed too red and swollen. She bit her lower lip and groaned, finding it hard to raise herself to a sitting position without feeling a little bit of pain.

"We are no longer in the shed, are we?" She asked.

I shook my head and glanced around the room. Everywhere was properly lit. There was a pleasing fragrance too while a soft breeze blew in from the opened windows. There was a shelf beside the window that had a jug and glass cups atop it. The bed we sat on was well-dressed and fluffy too, making it seem as if the entire room was prepared for comfort and nothing else.

I suspected that we were exactly where Tuya said that we would be. I was surprised though, expecting that we would be in a home far worse than the four corners of the shed we had lived in for almost six years. I was also frightened since our fate was still unknown. But at least I still had Cyril, I consoled myself. If nothing could be done to revive her the night before, I probably would think of ending a foreseen loneliness with my own hands.

I had thought of suicide once or twice in the past too. It was always after I had been beaten by clients who loved to inflict pain on children even while they raped them. One particular man, despite being Mongolian as I was, had tied me to the bed and commanded me to lie on my chest, while he tore my back with various strikes of a whip. He licked the blood off afterward and resumed the torture all over again. When he finally decided to penetrate my thighs, he squeezed my neck hard and choked me.

He left when he was done without even a backward glance. He wasn't the first to treat me as such. I felt like a piece of garbage. I cried until my voice was gone. I thought about how I was young and going through a lot. I wanted to end it all, but I just couldn't. I always thought I would return home one day. Tuya would give us our freedom when the time was right, and she would also help us to find our way back home. This drove me every time.

But now...now, I wasn't even sure we would ever see Tuya. If we were really in Bangkok, she doesn't want us to ever find our way back to her. It was the reason we were drugged before leaving the shed.

"I think someone is at the door, Yuna!"

I jolted out of my thoughts and found myself holding on tight to Cyril's wrist. She cringed in pain, but I wouldn't let go. It was the first time I would be in another terrain ever since I escaped from my first captors.

The door into the room eventually jerked open, more light slithering into the room. A burly man stood in the middle of the light, holding a wide object in his hand. He looked dangerous at first and Cyril and I shuddered backward, expecting that the worst thing could happen to us. When he stepped slowly into the room though, I noticed with a soft sigh that he held only a tray with food in his hands.

He stepped slowly towards us, his face becoming clearer. He wasn't exactly a man, I thought afterward. He looked quite young – probably eighteen – with curly black hair and a pointed nose. Half of his face looked weird though as if the skin had healed from a gruesome fire burn. He dropped the tray in front of us on the bed and stared at us for so long, I wasn't even aware I held my breath the entire time.

He looked vaguely familiar. He was exhaling hard when his eyes focused on me. He said nothing. He just stared at me as if he expected something from us. Or perhaps, he expected a reaction from me.

"Don't trust anyone, Yuna." He finally whispered. "Don't believe everything you see."

He stood and was gone before I could mutter any word. I was baffled and confused. Shut the door closed behind him as he exited, the loud noise jolting the hairs on my skin alive. Cyril glance at me surprised as well.

"You know him?" She asked.

Now, as my mind began to calculate the possibility of who he was, I wished he didn't look vaguely familiar. I wished the memories of my escape six years ago didn't just come back to me a while ago. If they hadn't, perhaps I would have thought that he was insane and probably worked for the man that had bought us from Tuya.

But these weren't the thoughts in my head. All I could think about were curly black hair, a pointed nose, and deep blue eyes.

Od. How did he survive all these years?

He was supposed to be dead.

CHAPTER SEVEN

Truth and Freedom

Cyril and I couldn't sleep throughout the entire night. We dozed off sometimes only to jolt awake whenever we heard the breeze blowing too hard or whenever we could hear footsteps outside the door.

No one came into the room anymore. We could hear people moving around the house, but we couldn't confirm what was happening around us. Unlike the typical moans or groans that echoed around Tuya's shed, we could only hear chatters and the sounds of laughter. The only time there was silence was late into the night and hours later, with little rays of the rising sun becoming apparent through the windows, the noise in the house was back up.

There was a click at the door eventually, but no one walked through the door for a few seconds. Eventually, a lanky man stepped in, dressed in a loose robe and looking like he was completely naked underneath.

"Oh well, aren't they exactly worth my money?" He grinned, staring at us admiringly.

His body moved fluidly and if half of his hairy flat chest wasn't showing, I would have thought he was female. He had shabby strands of beards too and seemed to be using a lot of cocaine. There was a speck of white powder on his wide mustache.

"Step forward, little one." He beckoned at us. "There is really nothing to frighten you about me."

Cyril and I didn't move. Cyril especially curled backward and seemed to be irritated by his presence.

"Well, that was expected." We heard him chuckle. "Tuya did tell me both of you would be a bit of trouble. Now, would you have me ask again or would you be nice enough to step forward as I have earlier asked."

There was something about his new tone that suggested that he wasn't a man to be crossed. He always got whatever he wanted too, and we would be foolish not to obey his orders.

"Now, good. Good girls." He grimaced as soon as we left the bed and coyly stepped towards him.

"You probably have heard of me." He said, "Tuya referred to me as Bat Erdene, yes?"

I nodded, remembering clearly how Tuya had told Hulagu about us being gone after he contacted a *Bat Erdene.*

"Oh, I expected that you would be the smart one." Bat Erdene smiled at me. "Yuna, correct?"

Again, I nodded, wondering how easily he could shift between being irritable to being frightening and nice. There was also that putrid smell that came from him as he spoke.

"Well, Yuna, what do you think about this room?" I heard him chuckle. "Would you like to have it all to yourself?"

I glanced around the room, pretending as if it was the first time I would be noting the light, the windows, the soft sheets, and the cupboard.

"At what price?" I whispered.

Bat Erdene seemed surprised. "Pardon?" He scoffed.

"At what price do we get it? Do we have to fuck men like we always do? Do we get fisted, beaten, drugged or do we just lay back silently and have all those done to us at the same time? A few months later, the room wouldn't be ours anymore, would it? – it would belong to a new set of girls?"

I asked the question so nonchalantly that even I was shocked by my own words. Bat Erdene took a step backward as if he wanted to take a good look of my face. Eventually, a wide smile spread over his face while he stepped forward and cupped one of my cheeks in his hand.

"Ohhh but I am so going to enjoy having you around." He hissed.

He hit my cheek swiftly and hard with the back of his palm, Cyril jerking forward with a furious groan. She stopped in her track though when she realized that I hadn't even reacted to the hit. I only smiled up at Bat Erdene, wondering the fury as well as the confusion that was going on in his head. He would, of course, realize that nothing would ever have us believe or trust him. The kind gestures of the first day are usually preceded by many hurt and betrayal. It was always like that with the people that had taken us in.

"I see you both don't feel pain." Bat Erdene scoffed now. "It is good for business."

He turned and began to head out of the room. When he paused at the door to take a final look at us, I noticed mischief spreading across his face like cancer. He was already cooking up various plans to break us, to hurt us. I knew this somehow.

"Enjoy the peace of my room for another day." He whispered as he stepped out and closed the door behind him. "Bangkok is different from Chiang Rai.

You will learn a lot by being on the streets here. Oh, you will."

I came to know Bangkok as the most populous city in Thailand that I had ever come across. It was overpopulated. The city streets were always busy with people and merchants, as well as fun lovers and Buddhists. It was amidst the city congestion that Bat Erdene had made a business of prostitution and trading of heroin and ecstasy for himself.

While he fed us twice on our second day in the city, two men walked into the room the next morning and threw some tops and short skirts at Cyril and me. We were then instructed to freshen up in the bathroom and wear any of the clothes that we liked. We understood immediately that we were about to carry out our first job in the city. We didn't just have a clue if things would be so different to the activities we were already used to.

They turned out to be different after all. The men made sure we were dressed like ordinary Thailand girls with a small bag or backpack, heading to work or to school. One of them left and came back with another girl who looked our age and instructed her to help us fix our hair into ponytails. Afterward, they guided us out of the room, leading us into a more beautiful part of the house and up the stairs to meet Bat Erdene.

Bat Erdene clapped gleefully when he noticed us. He was surrounded by two other men and since the night Od brought food to our room, it was the first time I was seeing him again. He stood beside Bat Erdene, his face devoid of any emotion. He didn't reveal any reaction to show that he knew who I was.

"Don't they look amazing, uhm Od? They will be perfect to fool the boys in brown, won't they?"

Od only nodded. He bent to pick up two bags on a nearby table and placed each one in our hands.

"What are we supposed to do with them?" Cyril asked.

"Oh please. You should learn to be patient. It is how anyone ever survives or become successful in new places." Bat Erdene muttered. He nodded at Od though who once more picked another bag from the table, pulled out two papers and gave them to us.

"Not to worry. It is just a map of every single street, building and public transport in Bangkok." Bat Erdene grinned when he noticed the confusion on our faces. "You should notice the yellow dots starting from a point in the city to your destination. All you have to do is get there, give the bags to whoever receives you and then find your way to the starting point. You are not to ever concern yourself with the contents of the bag."

I was more confused. I frowned, wondering why we were being given the freedom to walk around the city. Didn't Bat Erdene consider the possibility of his errand girls running away? Contacting local authorities was out of it anyway. Living with Tuya had taught me how unhelpful they can be since they probably can be paid off.

Bat Erdene was able to see through the frown on my face. He stepped forward, standing just beside Od. "I have eyes everywhere." He said. "Don't even think about not getting to your destination. You wouldn't like the outcome of such insolence. You do not have legal documents of your stay in this city. You are nobody and if the authorities cannot make you disappear, I can."

In that instant, I notice Od nodding gently. He seemed to be telling me to believe Bat Erdene's threat. The nod was so brief and almost unnoticeable though that I was unsure I had seen it. I, however, gulped in a breath and nodded at Bat Erdene's words. Cyril did the same thing, bringing a smile to Bat Erdene's lips.

"Now, be gone." He said, waving his hand dismissively. "Od and Batu here would drive you to your starting point and they would also get you when you are back there."

I thought Bat Erdene referred to Cyril and me, but it appeared to be the opposite. The men that had led us out of the room earlier simply stepped aside, one of them holding on to Cyril's shoulder. Batu was the second man in the room with Bat Erdene. He stepped forward with Od, both men leading me down the stairs and away from Cyril. Cyril's gaze dropped to the floor with disappointment as I was led away while my breaths dropped in sadness.

Whatever new world we had just stepped in, it was about to create a distance between Cyril and me.

$$*****$$

I did exactly what I was told to do the first few weeks of my stay in Bangkok. Bat Erdene's operation was simple, tactical and safe. He housed so many young girls in various parts of Bangkok, only offering them food and shelter as payment for their services. Apart from delivering hard drugs to various locations, he also sent some of the girls to clients' homes for sex. The clients paid in advance and have the right to any choice of sexual intercourse with the girls when they arrived.

The first week for me was just about delivering bags to certain locations. The map always helped. Once I was dropped off by Od and Batu, the map helped me to locate buildings, temples, shores, streets and public transports. In the end, I might get to a safe house, a private property or an avenue with mean-looking men who were always in a hurry to collect the bag from me, go through the content to see that it was exactly what they wanted and disperse within seconds.

"Who are the boys in brown?" I once asked Batu when he came to drive me back to the house. "The men I give the bags to sometimes speak of them with fear. Bat Erdene once mentioned them too."

My naiveté seemed to crack Batu up. "The Thai police." He chuckled. "You haven't seen them in their brown attire? Let's just say they don't like to see whatever is in your brown bag on some certain set of people."

Batu answered my question but he also confirmed my suspicions ever since my first job. I had become part of a group that boldly committed a crime in the city. I didn't have a choice. I also had Od who hardly ever spoke to me. Sometimes, I wonder if it wasn't just my imagination that I knew who he was. I never got a chance to ask him questions, either. I wanted to know if he knew what had happened to the rest of us. Was he also found underneath a heap of sand as I was?

One month eventually went by and I got used to all the streets and transport system of Bangkok. I didn't need the map anymore. Meanwhile, I somehow realized that every movement I took around the city had been monitored too. There were men who stared at me at various points whenever I was on my way to deliver a package. At first, I thought they were dangerous but seeing that they never stepped forward to attack or arrest me, I soon realized that they worked for Bat Erdene too. I was right to think that he wasn't a man to be crossed. He was also extraordinarily careful and tactical with his operations.

By the fifth month of my stay in Bangkok, I was already familiar with a few other girls that worked for Bat Erdene. Most of them weren't always around the house. It was as if they worked round the clock, having gotten more familiar with the business and the city. Cyril and I worked more as time went by too, getting us neck-deep in the business. At some point, we were sent to meet clients that wanted both the drugs and young girls to fuck. We let this happen without complaint and get back to our picking points, ready for another working day.

This would have proceeded forever if I hadn't come across Altantsetseg at a warehouse two weeks later. I had thought she and her sister, Chinua, were dead too.

The warehouse was a storeroom for toys and beads and was also my destination for a next delivery. I noticed that the men this time around weren't up to fleeing the scene, immediately I handed the bag to them. One of the men had also come with a girlfriend who had half of her face covered with a black scarf. She immediately whispered into her lover's ears and exited towards a restroom after taking a long weird look at me.

I felt inclined to follow her. So, I asked the men if I could use the restroom while they confirmed that everything in the bag was intact. I only got a few grunts as a reply, having no choice than to leave at my own request.

Stepping into the restroom, I came face to face with Altantsetseg, her once-soft cheeks having grown to have hard edges. She smiled curtly at me before running towards me to give me a warm embrace.

"Oh, Altantsetseg!" I cried. "Whatever happened to you all these years? You were caught and sold off? I thought you, Khulan, Chinua, Od and the rest were dead."

"Only Od, Chinua and I ever made it through that night." I heard Altantsetseg whisper. She held back tears and stepped back to take a long look at me. "You have seen Od I suppose?" she asked.

"We don't have much time." She whispered when I nodded. "How long have you been in Bangkok?"

"Ten months. A year?" I told her.

"And you aren't dead or resold yet." She whispered as if that was good news to her. "You probably didn't think to run or disobey Bat Erdene then. You have always been the extra lucky one."

"What are you talking about?" I asked her.

"Ten months is enough to get the dogs off your back. You wouldn't be watched as often as you have always been in the past."

"Is that how you got out after you were brought here?" I asked, finally having guesses of what she spoke of. "Are you out?"

"I was." I heard her whisper.

"You were caught? Why are you back?"

"You don't understand." She replied. "Some of us made it out, for good. A few of us weren't so lucky. Dead, they are after they were caught. Dead. Others must treat sexually transmitted diseases and addiction to drugs. We were already broken beyond repair."

Altantsetseg was driving me nuts. She was muttering words so fast it was hard to keep up. She kept staring at the door as if she expected someone to barge through it soon. I held her hand suddenly, utterly curious about some of the girls that had made it out, as she had phrased.

"Tell me about those that got out," I told her. "How? Where are they?"

"Phuket." Altantsetseg sighed, temporarily calm. "I was there too. We were so happy. Some of us got work, decent work at restaurants and bars, but payment was just food and shelter. I wanted more."

"So, you came back here and got back to the men that probably raped or forced you to use the drugs you once sold to them?"

"It is better this way," Altantsetseg argued. "I was of no use despite the freedom in Phuket. Many us went back to Mongolia to find our parents too. Everything was just so wrong. They didn't want us back. We learned so many things when we became free. We have been lied to since we were taken. So many lies."

"I don't understand," I whispered. "What did you find out?"

"We were sold by our own parents, Yuna," Altantsetseg whispered. A tear finally fell down her cheeks. "Father only had two daughters and he sold us off like animals to have enough money to cater for the boys."

Luke. G. Dahl

I was shell-shocked. In an instant, I was back to the
fields in front of my father's house again. I could
remember clearly what had happened now. It wasn't
my imagination anymore. I wasn't falling into a dark
pit. Everything was as clear as the day. The strong
hands that had gripped my hands first were Father's.
He had quickly passed me on to stronger arms that
immediately left the house, Father only standing there
while I was taken away. His figure had been the
silhouette of my dreams. He had sold me off,
condemning me to a fate that had broken every ounce
of my spirit.

"I was only eight years old." I found myself muttering.
"I was only eight years old."

I was backing away from Altantsetseg. She tried to hold
my hand, but I wouldn't let her. I inhaled and exhaled
with difficulty. My heart was beating fast and I could
feel a sudden ache in my head. It couldn't be the truth,
I tried to convince myself but deep down, I felt that it

was. I always knew. I just never wanted the truth to be so dwindling.

"Where will you go? Yuna!"

I wasn't even aware that I was running. I hurried into the warehouse once more, staring absentmindedly at the men who only nodded at me to show their satisfaction with the content of the bag.

I didn't stop to say anything to them. I only reduced my pace and stepped out into the afternoon sun, thinking of all the years of suffering and pain. I thought about the number of times I had been raped and abused. It had all begun that afternoon...the day I was kidnapped, and Father had made it happen.

I began to run once more, far away from the point I was supposed to return to for pickup.

I was never going back to Bat Erdene. Never.

EPILOGUE

"So, that is everything – my entire tale. You should know some part of it since you were in it."

Od sat in front of me, his eyes revealing nothing as usual. He must have perfected the act over the years. He had been the one to find me since I ran a week ago, always hiding from plain sight and seeking secret passage to anywhere else but Bangkok or Mongolia.

When he stepped into the small hidden shed that had become my home for a week two hours ago, I had no inkling to run. I had only poured two cups of tea, handed one to him, and sat. When he took the cup and sat on the chair across mine, I had begun my tale then, recounting my ordeal from the moment it had all began.

He had said nothing the entire time. I knew he listened though, for his blue eyes never left mine. His scarred face sometimes got me curious, but I knew better than to ask him now what had happened all those years.

"So, what now?" I asked. "Are you here to take me back to Bat Erdene, or are you here to kill me upon his request?"

His silence was making me nervous. When he moved, I thought he would reach for my neck or drive a knife through my heart, but he did nothing. He only dropped the empty cup in his hand on a nearby stool and smiled.

"Leave during the night." He whispered. "There will be a bus moving out of the city around ten. Some of its passengers, Cyril inclusive, have been through a lot like you. Don't miss it."

He was leaving and all I could do was stare at his back while my eyes filled with tears.

"It was you. You have always planned an escape." I finally managed to whisper. "It was you who got them all out one after the other. Why didn't you ever leave yourself? Why?"

He paused at the door, the smile on his face dissolving into profound sadness.

"Use your freedom," he muttered, "if you ever have a peaceful one, to find others like us. Perhaps you can tell them the same tale you told me today."

He was gone in a blink of an eye. I was alone in the shed and once more, the entire years of slavery flashed through my eyes.

I wept uncontrollably.

Daddy's Curse 2

An Od Life
A Young Boy Who Has Survived Child Slavery
Remembers...

Get Your Hands on This E-Book & Find Out Today!

If you would like to sign up for my newsletter, please visit
www.cedenheim.com

Luke. G. Dahl

"Word-of-mouth is crucial for any author to succeed.

If you enjoyed the book, please leave a review on my <u>Amazon review page</u>, even if it is just a sentence or two. It would make all the difference"

Made in the USA
Columbia, SC
11 February 2019